AND WHEN WE PRAY

The Prayer Warrior's Workbook

Dr. Phyllis Glass

KP PUBLISHING COMPANY

Copyright 2020 by Dr. Phyllis Glass

All rights reserved. In accordance with the U.S. Copyright Act of 1976, the scanning, uploading, and electronic sharing of any part of this book without the permission of the publisher is unlawful piracy and theft of the author's intellectual property. If you would like to use material from this book (other than for review purposes), prior written permission must be obtained by contacting the publisher at info@knowledgepowerinc.com.

Thank you for your support of the author's rights.

ISBN: 978-1-950936-69-4 (Paperback)
ISBN: 978-1-950936-89-2 (Ebook)
Library of Congress Control Number: 2020920455

Editor: Frank Williams
Cover Design: Juan Roberts, Creative Lunacy
Interior Design: Jennifer Houle
Literary Director: Sandra Slayton James

Published by:

KP Publishing Company
Publisher of Fiction, Nonfiction & Children's Books
Valencia, CA 91355
www.kp-pub.com

Printed in the United States of America

Contents

Introduction	*vii*
CHAPTER 1: Meaning and Purpose of Prayer	1
CHAPTER 2: Importance of Prayer	5
CHAPTER 3: Praying in the Spirit	9
CHAPTER 4: Secrets to Answered Prayer	13
CHAPTER 5: Tools to Use in Battle	17
CHAPTER 6: Prayers are Personal	23
CHAPTER 7: How to Build and Record Your Own Prayers	27
CHAPTER 8: Build and Record Your Own Prayer Progress	43
Bibliography	*53*
About the Author	*55*

Introduction

This workbook is a supplement to and intended to be used in conjunction with book: *And When We Pray: The Prayer Warriors Weapons of Warfare*.

The purpose is for new and seasoned Christians within a classroom and/or individual study environment to further increase knowledge and understanding of the purpose and power of prayer.

This book contains questions directly related to the textbook and may provide additional clarity and understanding. This workbook also seeks to achieve the following goals and objectives:
- Increased knowledge and understanding of the purpose and power of prayer.
- Learn how to construct a prayer with the confidence of receiving an answer
- It will allow the reader to work at their pace.
- Provides an opportunity to absorb content on a more in-depth level through the process of the answering questions from each chapter.
- Provide an opportunity to apply critical thinking skills through the application of using "Thoughts and Notes" entries to reflect on lessons learned.
- Outlines portions of the text in a more interesting and exciting way.
- Each chapter provides hands on activity that allows for a more engaged method of learning.
- Workbook documents evidence of continued progress after each chapter.

Answer the following questions from each chapter and document what you were able to glean most from that chapter.

CHAPTER 1

Meaning and Purpose of Prayer

1. What are the requirements of a proper prayer?

AND WHEN WE PRAY

2. Match the correct word(s) that more closely aligns with the definition provided below:

_____ a. Regretful, contrite, remorseful, repentant

_____ b. Confidence, assurance, conviction, sureness

_____ c. Exalt, salute, pay homage to, recognition

_____ d. Faithfulness, dedication, reverence, worship

_____ e. Appreciative, thankful, sense of obligation

_____ f. Mediate, negotiate, beseech, appeal

_____ g. Inquire, pray, petition, entreat

Faith/Trust   Thanksgiving/Gratefulness

Adoration/Devotion   Supplication/Petition

Confession/Contrition   Intercession/Request

Praise/Tribute

3. According to Romans 15:30-33, what specific request did Apostle Paul ask of the Roman Christians?

　　_____

4. In the model prayer, whose will do we obey?

　　_____

5. Name each person of the Holy Trinity and their specific function.

　　Person　　　　　　　　　Function

　　_____　　　　　_____

　　_____　　　　　_____

　　_____　　　　　_____

6. What is the most important thing you learned from Chapter 1?

　　_____

　　_____

　　_____

　　_____

　　_____

Chapter 1: Thoughts and Notes   Date: _____

What did you benefit most from after reading Chapter 1?

_____

_____

_____

_____

_____

What did you benefit most from after completing the Q&A in Chapter 1?

_____

_____

_____

_____

_____

CHAPTER 2

Importance of Prayer

1. This chapter confirms that God hears everybody's prayer.

   True ____ False ____

2. According to 1 Peter 5:10, what four blessings can we expect to experience?

   a. _____

   b. _____

   c. _____

   d. _____

3. What is the term used to describe our freedom to choose our own destiny?

_____

4. Name at least three ways we can quench the Holy Spirit:

a. _____

_____

b. _____

_____

c. _____

_____

5. Name the six-fold parts of the Christian armor:

a. _____

b. _____

c. _____

d. _____

e. _____

f. _____

6. What is the most important thing you were able to learn from Chapter 2?

Chapter 2: Thoughts and Notes   Date: _____

What did you benefit most from after reading Chapter 2?

_____

_____

_____

_____

_____

What did you benefit most from after completing the Q&A in Chapter 2?

_____

_____

_____

_____

_____

CHAPTER 3

Praying in the Spirit

1. Praying in the Spirit is a characteristic of human nature.

True ____ False ____

2. Name at least 3 benefits to praying in the Spirit.

a. _____

b. _____

c. _____

3. Who distributes the gifts of the Spirit? _____

_____

_____

_____

_____

4. Name the nine Gifts of the Spirit?

1. _____

2. _____

3. _____

4. _____

5. _____

6. _____

7. _____

8. _____

9. _____

5. What are the most important thing you learned from Chapter 3?

_____

_____

_____

_____

_____

Chapter 3: Thoughts and Notes   Date: _____

What did you benefit most from after reading Chapter 3?

_____

_____

_____

_____

_____

What did you benefit most from after completing the Q&A in Chapter 3?

_____

_____

_____

_____

_____

CHAPTER 4

Secrets to Answered Prayer

1. Complete this verse: Now _____ is the substance of things _____ for, the _____ of things not seen.

2. Write one scripture that indicates that there are conditions to answered prayer:

   _____

   _____

   _____

   _____

3. Fasting is one of the pillars of the Christian faith.

   True ___ False ___

4. Give at least five reasons why most prayers are not answered:

    a. _____

    b. _____

    c. _____

    d. _____

    e. _____

5. Every person will be saved whether they confess their sins or not.

    True ____ False ____

6. What is the most important thing you learned from Chapter 4?

    _____

    _____

    _____

    _____

    _____

    _____

Chapter 4: Thoughts and Notes   Date: _____

What did you benefit most from after reading Chapter 4?

_____

_____

_____

_____

_____

What did you benefit most from after completing the Q&A in Chapter 4?

_____

_____

_____

_____

_____

CHAPTER 5

Tools to Use in Battle

1. What scripture references the three essential parts of an effective prayer? _____

2. What are the three essential parts of an effectual fervent prayer?

   a. _____

   b. _____

   c. _____

3. What scripture commands people to humble themselves and pray, seek the face of God, turn from their wicked ways before He hears from heaven?

   _____
   _____
   _____
   _____

4. 2 Corinthians 10:4 tells us we can expect victory when we use these four weapons of warfare:

   a. _____

   b. _____

   c. _____

   d. _____

5. In this spiritual fight, we don't wrestle with flesh and blood, but against:

   a. _____

   b. _____

   c. _____

   d. _____

6. **What Fruit of the Spirit closely aligns with the definitions provided below?**

_____ a. Brotherly love that seeks the welfare of others

_____ b. One who is virtuous, generous, God-like in life and conduct

_____ c. Trait that shows confidence in God and His faithfulness

_____ d. One who shows strength while in a weakened position

_____ e. Expresses joy that is not the result of anything we've done for ourselves

_____ f. One who endures challenges and offences without murmuring

_____ g. One who is able to exercise self-control of the flesh

_____ h. When we feel safety and security regardless of circumstances

_____ i. One whose disposition is soft-spoken, even tempered

Love	Joy	Gentleness
Meekness	Peace	Kindness
Temperance	Longsuffering	Faith

7. What is the most important thing you learned from Chapter 5?

Chapter 5: Thoughts and Notes   Date: _____

What did you benefit most from after reading Chapter 5?

_____

_____

_____

_____

_____

What did you benefit most from after completing the Q&A in Chapter 5?

_____

_____

_____

_____

_____

CHAPTER 6

Prayers are Personal

1. Who petitioned God to save the people of Sodom and Gomorrah?

_____

2. To gain the favor of God, what are ten commands that we should follow:

1. _____

2. _____

3. _____

4. _____

5. _____

6. _____

7. _____

8. _____

9. _____

10. _____

3. **What are the seven ways outlined in James 1:4-8 to get an answer to prayer:**

   1. _____

   2. _____

   3. _____

   4. _____

   5. _____

   6. _____

   7. _____

4. **What is the most important thing you learned from Chapter 6?**

   _____

   _____

   _____

   _____

   _____

   _____

# Chapter 6: Thoughts and Notes	Date: _____

What did you benefit most from after reading Chapter 6?

_____

_____

_____

_____

_____

What did you benefit most from after completing the Q&A in Chapter 6?

_____

_____

_____

_____

_____

CHAPTER 7

How to Build and Record Your Own Prayer

Now for putting your own personal prayers to work in three easy steps remembering key instructions from Scripture:

Jesus saith unto him, I am the way, the truth, and the life: no man cometh unto the Father, but by me. If ye had known me, ye should have known my Father also: and from henceforth ye know him, and have seen him.

JOHN 14:6-7

This passage shows us that none shall come to the Father except through Jesus Christ. We must remember to acknowledge Jesus Christ as our personal savior because He is the advocate between the Father and us.

1. Start With Giving Thanks to God

Always start with giving God thanks for what you know He's done for you. Actually, take pen to paper and make a list of what He's done for you. Start with a short prayer, and make it personal to include some of the obvious examples of blessings as follows

    a. Thank God for waking you up this morning, with a reasonable portion of health and strength.
    Prayer: Lord I give thanks that you work me up this morning with a reasonable portion of health and strength. I thank you for keeping

me through the night. I pray you continue to watch over me. In Jesus name I pray.

b. For what some consider the simple things of life, the food on your table, the roof over your head,
   Prayer: Lord I thank you for the food on my table, the roof over my head. I give thanks for the resources that you provided, for I know that you are THE SOURCE. I ask that you continue to give me favor as I provide for my family. I ask this prayer in the name of Jesus. Amen.

c. For the parents or guardians, He's assigned to care, nurture, train and guide you,
   Prayer: Father which art in heaven, I thank you for my mother and father. I give thanks that you assigned them to raise and nurture me. For them living according to your word to train me up in the way that I should go. I pray for my parents that they might continue on in good health. Protect our home and us. I ask this pray in Jesus name. Amen.

d. For the wonderful children He's blessed you with
   Prayer: Lord I thank you for blessing me with my children. I pray you will send your angels before and after them, protecting them from all manner of hurt harm and danger when they leave this house. Let nothing come near them to distract them from your will and word as you direct their paths. I ask this prayer in the name of Jesus. Amen.

e. For being THE SOURCE, for the job(s) that have opened up to bring resources and provisions to your household.
   Prayer: Father God, I give thanks for the job you've blessed me with. I know how important it is to take care of my family and myself. I thank God this income has provided me with enough to pay my tithes and still take care of my family. I thank you for keeping the cankerworm away, and continually open doors for all my finances to be taken care of. I pray this prayer in the precious Name of Jesus.

f. For being the provider of all things, He's made possible on your behalf
    Prayer: I give thanks this day O Lord, for you being the provider of all things. Because of you I see all things are possible, and I see the results of my prayers being answered. I thank you for the favor you've given me as you open doors on my behalf and make every crooked way straight. I'll remember to bless you each day I awaken as I ask these prayers in Jesus name. Amen.

g. For the angels He's dispatched for your protection on a daily basis as you travel on the highways, byways and skyways.
    Prayer: Lord God, I give thanks for the love and protection you have provided me every day as I travel on the highways, byways and skyways. I pray your angels continue to watch over me in all of my going out and coming in, and in my rising each morning and going to sleep at night. I give thanks that you see fit to give my family traveling mercy each day. If I had ten-thousand tongues, I couldn't thank you enough for what you've done for me. I pray you continue to lead and guide me on the path of righteousness. I ask these prayers in the matchless name of Jesus.

While the examples above offer short and simple prayers, do not underestimate how powerful they can be. These prayers can be prayed singularly or combined, depending on how you choose to apply your signature style of praying to God in conjunction with how the Holy Spirit will lead and guide you.

Using the prayer samples above, start by writing in the space provided after this section, in your own words, a similar prayer. If more space is needed, use a page at the back of this workbook. You'll find once you get started, a flood of things will come to mind that you can communicate to God that you are thankful for.

2. Ask According To His Will
Be sure what you're asking God for is within His will according to His word. Here are a few prayer requests that may be associated with Scripture.

AND WHEN WE PRAY

    a. Lord increase my territory when looking for new opportunities, as Jabez did.

And Jabez was more honourable than his brethren; and his mother called his name Jabez saying, Because I bare him with sorrow. And Jabez called on the God of Israel saying, Oh that thou wouldest bless me indeed, and enlarge my coast, and that thine hand might be with me, and that thou wouldest keep me from evil, that it may not grieve me! And God granted him that which he requested.

1 Chronicles 4:9-10

Using the prayer of Jabez as a reference is important because it demonstrates how our request should be specific when we present them to God in prayer. Jabez asked God to:

1. Bless me indeed
2. Enlarge my coast or territory
3. Let Your hand be with me
4. Keep me from evil
5. Keep me from grief

Those five requests are some of the usual request that most of us go to God for. This scripture also tells us that God granted Jabez with those things he requested. All throughout the Bible are instances where God answered prayer. This proves that God will honor our prayer when we pray in His will. What God does for one, he will do for another, because according to Romans 2:11 God is not a respector of persons.

    b. Lord allow my path to cross and connect with those you've placed in my life that will help me to learn, grow, and prosper.

Trust in the Lord with all thine heart; and lean not unto thine own understanding. In all thy ways acknowledge him, and he shall direct thy paths.

Proverbs 3:5-6

Give, and it shall be given unto you; good measure, pressed down, and shaken together, and running over, shall men give into your bosom. For with the same measure that ye mete withal it shall be measured to you again.

LUKE 6:38

In this verse, Jesus gives insight into the universal principle of "give and it will be given unto you. Here He teaches that if we are generous and unselfish ourselves, then we will be met with the same generosity from others. It refers in part to the Law of Reciprocity or reaping what you sow. When we give to others, or perform acts of kindness, or show concern for others, by principle, that attitude will be reflected back to the one that gives. What we get in return for our giving does not always come back in material things. This scripture also can reflect on our giving of tithes and offerings.

   c. Lord continue to bless my household with prosperity in health and in finances.

Honour the Lord with thy substance and with the first fruit of all thine increase: Shall shall thy barns be filled with plenty, and thy presses shall burse out with new wine.

PROVERBS 3:9-10

   d. Lord continue to keep me daily that I might walk in your wisdom and be a witness to others.

Get wisdom, get understanding; forget it not: neither decline from the words of my mouth.

PROVERBS 4:5

3. When Prayer Is New To You

If praying is relatively new to you, utilize the list below to get to know each person that make up the Holy Trinity are, and expand your prayer from there. A sincere prayer can be 5 minutes, 10-15 minutes or more. It's the content that is important.

It's all up to you and the time you choose to spend with God. Remember to make prayer a priority in your life.

Don't be afraid to add daily or weekly to your original prayer. Prayer usually starts with what I refer to as a "selfish" prayer because it only includes those things and people that affect our immediate circle. We are free to expand our prayer by including others, our church family and all those that could have an impact on our daily existence. We pray for our pastors who are charged with watching over all members of the church. We pray for our community, our teachers at school, and world events. There are many situations outside of our own circle that could have an impact on our households such as on our jobs or in the workplace. As you enhance your prayers, you'll l find you have developed prayers full of the unique personality God has blessed you and only you with. God knows your voice, your style of prayer, and based on that personal relationship you have established with God, He will remember you. We become prayer warriors as we make a significant difference in our lives and the lives of those around us.

Prayer should be open, honest, from the heart, sincere, specific. Drawing upon the character and description of the Person of the Trinity will determine how your prayer will be delivered. First, keeping in mind the scripture John 14:6 states that "none shall come to the Father except by me." The prayer should acknowledge Jesus Christ at all times. Unless of course, the prayer is in the spirit, in which case God the Father hears from you directly. So then, we're asking Jesus to carry our pray to the Father, with confidence that prayer is in His will according to 1 John 5:12-15) it might be answered in due season.

1 John
>*These things have I written unto you that believe on the name of the Son of God; that ye may now that ye have eternal life, and that ye may believe on the name of the Son of God.*
>
> *And this is the confidence that we have in him, that, if we ask anything according to his will, he hearth us;*
>
> *And if we know that he hears us, whatsoever we ask, we know that we have the petitions that we desired of him.*

There's Personality in Prayer:

In Chapter 6 of the book, And When We Pray: The Prayer Warrior Weapons of Warfare, you'll find sufficient examples of what others prayed for and why and includes those of Jesus himself. In those prayers, we can see the emotion, the sincerity and the desperation of those that prayed. Although Jesus prayed often, some of us seem to muster up a prayer only when things are not going well every day. We should pray at all times and without ceasing as instructed rather than waiting for a crisis to arise.

From the individual circumstances that Jarius, Moses, Hannah, Solomon, and Jesus experienced, we can get an idea of how to structure our prayers to God. Utilizing your own specific trials or tribulation, your own individual situation or circumstance, you can call on God to meet your need. Remember to be specific in your request and pray the will of God because His Word is His mind and will concerning each of us.

It's important to know that if you are leading someone else in prayer, offer a prayer based on what you know about the word of God. Do not agree with someone just because they ask you to, unless you know for sure that according to scripture, it's a general request meant for all.

Examples of prayers that would be within the general will of God are as follows: **Psalms 91**, I believe is one of the most effective scriptures in which to identify. Every verse seems to present a perfect place where you can insert your name and see a personal need to call upon my **Lord God**. This should be a fairly easy scripture to read, digest, meditate on, and make it a personal dedication. It is one where you can focus, read over and over until there is revelation into just how great God is and can be.

> **Prayer: Lord God on High**, I come before you boldly, acknowledging you as the maker of the heavens and the earth, giving thanks to you for hiding me when my enemies were near; providing for me a refuge in my day of trouble, being a fortress that no one or nothing could penetrate, protecting me at all times. My God, you have been a true

and faithful God to me. I put my trust in you, I feel secure knowing you are near.

The benefits of reading scripture and finding yourself in that scripture allows for a beautiful, heartfelt, personal prayer to go forth. When you see what God has done for others, know that he'll do the same for you providing you are in alignment with His will. It's important to remember that His Word is His will.

The following represent five common but specific experiences that most of us will encounter, or eventually want to acknowledge in prayer:

1. For a Job Opportunity:

Before you apply for a job opportunity or promotion, ask God to reveal if it's the right move for you. Talk it over with your wife (if married) beforehand so that you both agree it's in the best interest of the family. If that job is your hearts desire, let God know that you've prepared yourself and are qualified according to the requirements of the job assignment. Ask Him to open the hearts and minds of those who will determine the outcome of an interview. Continue to pray and wait on the Lord to open that door. We know God can do anything but fail. Don't assume that God did not hear your prayer, and don't assume God did not answer. If perhaps that door does not open, suffice it to say, God has something bigger in store for you. If you know without a doubt that you have aligned yourself with his principles, wait on God.

And let the beauty of the Lord our God be upon us: and establish thou the work of our hands upon us; yea, the work of our hands establish thou it.
                                                                                                PSALMS 90:17

Prayer: Father, God, I come to you in prayer because I know that you know me better than I know myself. I've prepared myself and believe in my heart that I'm well qualified to perform this job and ask that the Holy Spirit be with me during the interview process. I pray for a sense of peace and calm, that my mind is alert to answer any question given. I pray for favor with those who are charged with the selection process.

You said in your word, that whatsoever I ask, believing that I receive it, you would do it on my behalf. I pray this will be another opportunity to let my light shine, that you would get the glory as I ask this prayer in Jesus name. Amen.

2. On Marriage:

If you've met someone and feel marriage is on the horizon, pray with your mate and ask God to lead and guide you both. Be sure throughout the courtship you both are evenly yoked. You can't force someone to walk in Christ if they have not given their life over to Jesus. It's irresponsible to think that once you're married, things will change. Scripture says, "you'll know them by their fruit". If either person fails to walk in demonstrate of the Fruit of the Spirit; growth is still necessary. *Hebrews 13:4* says, "marriage is honourable in all", but unless both line up with the Word of God, or consider all that marriage involves, there's bound to be more strife than is necessary. You can't blame God if you follow your will instead of His. Pursue wise counseling through your Pastor or marriage counselor according to *Psalms 1:5*.

Therefore shall a man leave his father and his mother, and shall cleave unto his wife: and they shall be one flesh.

GENESIS 2:24

Let the husband render unto the wife due benevolence: and likewise also the wife unto the husband.

1 CORINTHIANS 7:3

Let nothing be done through strife or vainglory; but in lowliness of mind let each esteem other better than themselves.

PHILIPPIANS 2:3

Prayer: Dear God, I give thanks this day as I pray for peace, passion, purpose and prosperity for this marriage. I pray we both serve and honor you by keeping the statutes you have charged us with. We pray the power of the Holy Spirit as we strive for open and honest communication, and earnestly work through any adversities that may come against us. Give us the wisdom to build a healthy and spiritual union through you. Help us keep you in the center of all that we do; that our plans for the future are always according to your will for us. We thank you; we bless you, as we ask these prayers in the mighty name of Jesus. Amen.

3. On Anger:

There may be times when someone has said or done something to anger you. It can be a challenge not to react when you feel you have been physically or emotionally abused. Especially if it's from someone you are close to. But whether it's at home, work, or church, God has charged us with walking in a posture of holiness. Christians have a duty to let go of anger by forgiving those that trespass against us. We must remember as we expect God to forgive us, so shall we forgive others. That may take some practice and lots of prayer, but it must be done if we are to have peace. We pray and ask the Spirit to give us the strength that we don't have in the natural. Our prayer includes asking God to fill our lives with His perfect peace.

> *The discretion of a man deferreth his anger; and it is his glory to pass over a transgression*
>
> PROVERBS 19:11

> *Wherefore, my beloved brethren, let every man be swift to hear, slow to speak, show to wrath: For the wrath of man worketh not the righteousness of God.*
>
> JAMES 1:19-20

> *Be ye angry, and sin not, let not the sun go down upon your wrath.*
>
> EPHESIANS 4:26

Prayer: Almighty God, maker of the heavens and earth, hear my cry this day. Help me to control the anger that arises within me. Give me a since of peace and calm. Fill my heart with forgiveness toward those who have hurt me. Bring to my remembrance how I should walk in the Fruit of the Spirit that I may please you and not flesh. Touch the heart of even those who despitefully misuse me, that they, too, would have the mind of reconciliation. Lord, I bless my enemies that they might learn to walk in righteousness. I thank you for the access you have given me to walk in holiness. Heal my heart today, that I am able to have joy and not regret. I ask this prayer in Jesus name. Amen.

4. On Confusion:

There are many events in life where you may have some difficulty in making a decision or choice in which way to go. There will be lots of challenges throughout life that require us to take a thoughtful approach. Many of the decisions have impact that will affect us for years to come. So, we must be sure we use wisdom in everything we do, especially if it can have lasting consequences or repercussions. Unfortunately, many of us hesitate to come to God because we're ashamed or embarrassed that we couldn't figure it out on our own. But that's the perfect time to get God involved because we can pray for clarity in the middle of our confusion. That's what God expects for us to do. Only God has all the answers to everything at all times. God is looking for us to seek Him for answers. He knows the enemy would like to keep us in a state of confusion at all times if he could.

Likewise the Spirit also helpeth our infirmities; for we know not what we should pray for as we ought: but the Spirit itself maketh intercession for us with groanings which cannot be uttered. And he that searcheth the hearts knoweth what is the mind of the Spirit; because he maketh intercession for the saints according to the will of God.

ROMANS 8:26-27

For God is not the author of confusion, but of peace, as in all churches of the saints.

1 CORINTHIANS 14:33

Prayer: Dear Lord, I come before you praying you would open my eyes and heart to the decision before me. Cause my understanding to be aligned with your word and will for me. You said in your word you would never leave or forsake me; so, I'm asking you to reveal to me the path that you have designed specifically for me. I'm rebuking that spirit of confusion right now in the name of Jesus, and I declare my decision will be based on the clear knowledge that only God reveals to me. I will not be confounded or led astray because the Holy Spirit will lead and guide me in the right direction. I will not fear for God is with me. I give all thanks, glory and all praise to God the Father. I ask these prayers in the name of Jesus. Amen.

5. On Fear from the Past or Present:

Don't focus on fear; focus on what is true or real according to these Scriptures:

Finally, brothers, whatsoever things are true, whatsoever things are honest, whatsoever things are just, whatsoever things are pure, whatsoever things are lovely, whatsoever things are of good report, if there be any virtue, and if there be any praise, think on these   things.

PHILIPPIANS 4:8

Forget the former things; do not dwell on the past. See, I am doing a new thing! Now it springs up; do you not perceive it? I am making a way in the desert and streams in the wasteland,

ISAIAH 43:18-19

Examples of Prayers to God the Father

There are many names for God the Father with *Jehovah* probably being most recognized of those names used in church sermons, biblical studies or circles. It's important to know the meaning of those names and the purpose for how and/or why they are used. Knowing the meaning will help you formulate what it is you want God to do on your behalf.

> **Prayer: Father God**, I come before you this day in prayer. Hear me O **God of Israel**, Hear me O **God of David**. O **mighty God**. There is

no other that is able to look into my heart. As I profess that I trust in you, your Son, my **Lord and Savior Jesus Christ**, and in the **Holy Spirit** to lead and guide me into all righteousness. I pray that you will continue to make and mold me until I am completely what you have called me to be. These prayers I ask in your Son Jesus' name.

Prayer: Lord, help me as I strive to be the person you designed me to be, even before I was a seed in my mother's womb. For I know that you have pre-ordained and pre-destined my purpose even before the beginning of time. I pray to you **everlasting God** to help me present myself a better person on today and tomorrow than I was on yesterday. You have told me in *Psalm 139:14 that I am fearfully and wonderfully made: and marvelous are thy works; and that my soul knoweth right well*. I'll remember to give you all the glory, and honor, and praise as I ask these prayers in the name of **Jesus**.

By using the various names of all three persons of the Trinity, we learn to pray an effective, meaningful prayer with promise. See more prayers with other names of God.

Jehovah-Elohim

We know God as Jehovah Elohim—the **Eternal Creator** of Genesis 2:4-25

Prayer: Oh God, the Eternal creator of the heavens and the earth, have mercy on me as you did with Hannah, Jabez and Moses.

Jehovah-Jireh—The **Lord will see or provide** in Genesis 22:13-14

Prayer: Lord God, provide those things that I need to take care of my family and myself.

For the food for my table, a roof over our heads, and health to continue the work that provides for my family.

Jehovah-Nissi—The **Lord our banner**, a name given by Moses in Exodus 17:14-16 for the altar that he built to celebrate the defeat of the Amalekites.

Prayer: Almighty God, help me with the battle I face as you did with the Israelites in the battle against the Amalekites. I pray the strength of Jesus Christ to help me in my weakness. Stand with me in this struggle. I ask these prayers in the precious name of Jesus.

Prayers to God the Son
To Jesus Christ:

Prayer: My Lord and Savior Jesus Christ, I come in prayer that I might have an answer in due season. I come before you as filthy rags. Not deserving of your love except that you saw fit to seek me out. You knocked at my door and I answered. I am so thankful that you decided to take a chance on one who was flawed and carnal. I thank you for coming into my heart, cleaning me up, dusting me off until I was the picture of perfection in God's eyesight. That through you, I'm able to come before the throne of grace, asking what I desire in the Name of Jesus.

Prayer: I pray that you would strengthen me where I am weak, build me up where I've been torn down. Allow your **Holy Spirit** to lift me to a place of courageousness. For I know that **I am more than a conqueror**. I know that **I can do all things through Christ that strengthens me**. I Know that I am the above and not beneath. The head and not the tail. Help me to function in the manner in which you have **fearfully and wonderfully** made me. Help me get through this day with the joy only you can bring to my life. I ask these prayers in the powerful and matchless name of Jesus.

Some prayers we offer up to God will not be answered. Not because He doesn't hear you, but because as He said unto Paul "my grace is sufficient.

According to scripture, some trials and tribulations are meant for us to endure.

Here's two short prayers using other names for Jesus:

Prayer: Father God, I give thanks for your Son Jesus Christ, my Lord and Savior, for He is *(Psalm 62:2) my Rock and my salvation*; and I thank you for the life he gave at Calvary's cross that I might have a right to the tree of life. Continue to walk with me every day as I strive to learn your word, your will and your way. I pray in Jesus name. Amen.

Prayer: Jesus you mean so much to me. *(Isaiah 9:6)* You're called *Wonderful* because you've been marvelous to me; a *Counselor* because your word counsels and advise me to stay on a righteous path; The Mighty God because of the strength you provide me on a daily basis; *The everlasting Father* because there is no one like you, *The Prince of Peace* because you show us how to live without war and strife. And I give thanks to my heavenly Father for allowing me to be a joint-heir to the kingdom. I ask and pray you continually walk with me in the name of Jesus.

Know that according to scripture: None shall come by the Father except by me. We must acknowledge Jesus Christ as our personal savior because He is the advocate between the Father and us.

In my Father's house are many mansions: if it were not so, I would have told you. I go to prepare a place for you. And if I go and prepare a place for you, I will come again, and receive you unto myself; that where I am, there ye may be also. And whither I go ye know the way ye know. Thomas saith unto him, Lord, we know not whiter thou goest; and how can we know the way? Jesus saith unto him, I am the way, the truth, and the life: no man cometh unto the Father, but by me. If ye had known me, ye should have known my Father also: and from henceforth ye know him, and have seen him. Philip saith unto him, Lord, shew us the Father and it sufficeth us.

JOHN 14:2-8

Here are two short prayers using other names for Jesus:
Father God, I give thanks for your Son Jesus Christ, my Lord and Savior, for He is *(Psalm 62:2) my Rock and my salvation*; and I thank you for the life he gave at Calvary's cross that I might have a right to the tree of life. Continue to walk with me every day as I strive to learn your word, your will and your way. I pray in Jesus name. Amen.

Jesus you mean so much to me. *(Isaiah 9:6)* You're called *Wonderful* because you've been marvelous to me; a *Counselor* because your word counsels me; The mighty God because of the strength you provide; *The everlasting Father* because there is n one like you, *The Prince of Peace* because you show us how to live without war. And I give thank to my heavenly Father for being an heir to the kingdom. I ask and pray you continually walk with me in the name of Jesus.

Prayers to God the Holy Spirit
Jehovah-Rapha—Hebrew name for **Lord my Healer** in Exodus 15:26

    Prayer: Woman with the issue of blood.

Jehovah-Shalom—Hebrew for **Lord our Peace** in Judges 6:23-24 where an angel of the Lord came to Gideon and said "Peace be unto thee, fear not; thou shalt not die". And Gideon built an altar there unto the Lord and called it Jehovah-Shalom, which **according** to scripture is located at Ophrah of the Abiezrites. The word meaning peace, completeness, harmony, wholeness, prosperity, welfare and tranquility.

CHAPTER 8

Build and Record Your Own Prayer Progress

Date: _____

Let's start building those prayer.

Using the scripture provided (or find your own) you can start building your own prayers based on the research of that scripture and document those areas that have been personal to you and why.

Scripture:
The Rock (2 Samuel 22:32; Psalm 18:2)

Psalm 18:2, 31—Jehovah is my rock, and my fortress, and my deliverer, My God, my rock, in whom I will take refuge; my shield, and the horn of my salvation, and my high tower.

AND WHEN WE PRAY

Build and Record Your Own Prayer Progress

Using the scripture provided (or find your own) you can start building your own prayers based on the research of that scripture and document those areas that have been personal to you and why.

Scriptures:

Romans 11:26	The Deliverer
John 5:1-9	Your deliverer heals loneliness;
Luke 4:38-41	Removes sickness and obstacles;
Luke 4:33-36	Overpowers Demons;
Mark 4:35-41	Neutralizes nature's threats;
Acts 16:25-34	Breaks chains;
2 Peter 2:4-10	Overcomes trials and
2 Timothy 3:10-13	Strengthens in persecutions;
Galatians 5:1	Frees from Bondage to sin;
2 Corinthians 1:8-11	Saves from physical danger;
Hebrews 2:14-15	Erases fear of death

_____

_____

_____

_____

_____

_____

_____

_____

AND WHEN WE PRAY

Date: _____

Using the scripture provided (or find your own) you can start building your own prayers based on the research of that scripture and document those areas that have been personal to you and why.

Scripture:

_____

_____

_____

_____

_____

_____

_____

_____

_____

_____

Date: _____

Using the scripture provided (or find your own) you can start building your own prayers based on the research of that scripture and document those areas that have been personal to you and why.

Scripture:

_____

_____

_____

_____

_____

_____

_____

_____

_____

_____

_____

Thoughts and Notes Date: _____

Using the scripture provided (or find your own) you can start building your own prayers based on the research of that scripture and document those areas that have been personal to you and why.

Scripture:

_____

_____

_____

_____

_____

_____

_____

_____

_____

_____

_____

Thoughts and Notes Date: _____

Using the scripture provided (or find your own) you can start building your own prayers based on the research of that scripture and document those areas that have been personal to you and why.

Scripture:

_____

_____

_____

_____

_____

_____

_____

_____

_____

_____

_____

_____

Thoughts and Notes   Date: _____

Using the scripture provided (or find your own) you can start building your own prayers based on the research of that scripture and document those areas that have been personal to you and why.

Scripture:

_____

_____

_____

_____

_____

_____

_____

_____

_____

_____

Thoughts and Notes Date: _____

Using the scripture provided (or find your own) you can start building your own prayers based on the research of that scripture and document those areas that have been personal to you and why.

Scripture:

_____

_____

_____

_____

_____

_____

_____

_____

_____

_____

Bibliography

Dakes Annotated Reference Bible, Old and New Testaments of Authorized or King James Version Text by Finis Jennings Dake

About the Author

Dr. Phyllis Glass is an author of three books and a minister at Living Praise Christian Church for the Mature Adult Ministry in Palmdale, California. An ordained minister of the Gospel since 1993, she has conducted workshops and seminars for work and church for more than twenty-five years. Dr. Glass is filled with the Holy Ghost and speaks and teaches under the anointing of God.

Prior to becoming an author, she retired after ten years with the California State Department of Correction as a Credentialed Business Occupations Instructor; and twenty-three years of administration and business management in the aerospace sector. Dr. Glass holds a Doctor of Divinity degree and a Bachelor of Science degree in Business Administration. She is the mother of five adult children, two sons, three daughters, four grandsons, five granddaughters, and two great-grandchildren. Dr. Glass lives in Palmdale, California.

Other Books by Dr. Phyllis Glass

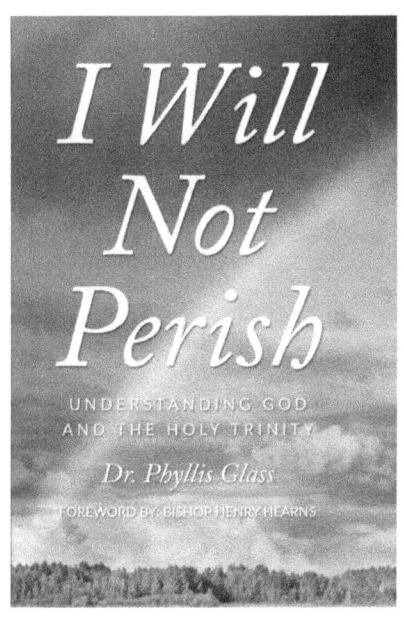 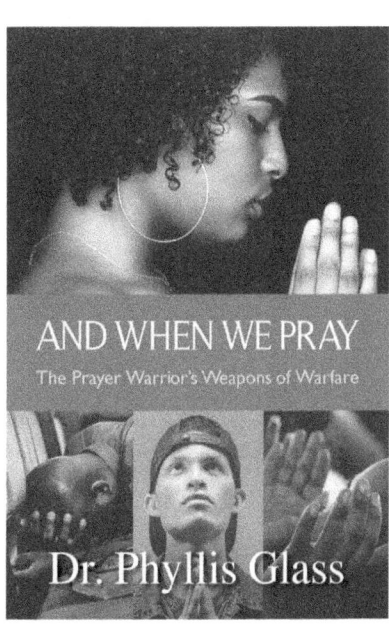